Spring Thrills!

By Jordan Avery

This is Cass.
She gets a thrill from spring!

Spring has lots of fun things.
Spring has things that are not so fun, too.

Cass likes to go on long walks in spring.

Look at this strip of buds that have sprung up!

Cass can spot a finch
on a spring walk.

She can spot a thrush on a strong branch.

Cass smells the spring plants with her nose.

She puts string on some sprigs from a shrub.

This bunch is for Cass's mum.

"I do not like spring plants,"
Min tells Cass.
"I must scrunch up my nose
and squint!"

That is not fun for Min.

Do you get a thrill from spring?

CHECKING FOR MEANING

1. List three reasons why Cass likes spring. *(Literal)*
2. What birds does Cass see on her spring walk? *(Literal)*
3. Do spring plants make Cass sneeze? *(Inferential)*

EXTENDING VOCABULARY

spring	How many sounds are in the word *spring*? How many syllables? What other words have the *spr* blend at the beginning? When is spring? What season comes after spring?
finch	What type of word is *finch*? What are the names of some other birds that you know?
sprigs	What is a sprig? What is another word the author could have used instead of *sprigs*?

MOVING BEYOND THE TEXT

1. Which season do you prefer: summer, autumn, winter or spring? Why?
2. Like Min, many people are bothered by the pollen from plants in spring because it causes allergies. Do pollen and dust affect you? Have you or anyone else you know ever had allergies to other things?
3. What are some other reasons people might need to stay indoors during particular seasons? Why?
4. What kinds of animals do you see in spring? Where would you see them?

SPEED SOUNDS

scr	str	spr	nch	squ
shr	thr			

PRACTICE WORDS